Boring Legal Stuff

The information and exercises provided in this book are designed to be informative and helpful for children with anxiety. This book is is not meant to be used, nor should it be used to diagnose or treat any physical or mental health condition. This book is not intended as a substitute for the medical advice of physicians. The publisher and author are not liable for any damages.

©2020 Lina Galanis.
All rights reserved.
ISBN:979-8627110721

No part of this work may be reproduced, stored in a retrieval system, or transmitted in any form or by any means, electronic, mechanical, photocopying, recording, or otherwise, without written permission.

NOTES ABOUT CONTENT

AGE RANGE: This book is intended for children aged 6-10. Please note that the large font size and areas for writing are reflective of that age group. To use this book properly, children should have a good grasp of reading and the ability the write sentences. The ideas expressed within are for any age.

COLOR: This book is published entirely in black and white with line drawings so that it can be colored like a coloring book. Coloring is a widely used relaxation technique and can be therapeutic for anxiety sufferers.

JOURNAL: If your child enjoys the 2 week journal at the end, please consider our companion book (**WORRY FREE ME JOURNAL**) that contains a full 6 month journal with additional weekly and monthly planning guides. Available exclusively at Amazon.

RELIGIOUS REFERENCE: According to research, people who are religious are happier than those who are not. Since religion plays a big part in so many people's lives, it would be a mistake not to include it in this book. As such, some parts of this book reference some people's belief in faith, prayer and a higher power.

How to Use this Book

This book is about anxiety and was created to help you with those troubling feelings. It is full of information and ways to help you feel better. Plus it is fun! You will get the most out of it if you start at the beginning and do the pages in order. Be honest with your answers.

Inside, you will find:

▷ stuff to think about

▷ questions to answer

▷ things to draw

▷ activities to do

▷ pictures to color,

like the ones on this page.

So make sure you have your pencils handy. We recommend using colored pencils, because some markers and pens may bleed through to the other side. There is a test page at the back so you can test your materials first. The pictures are all in black and white for you to color.

Let's get started!

Everyone worries, gets nervous or feels scared sometimes. It's completely

normal.

Those feelings are our brains' way of telling us that we might be in danger. If we never had those feelings we wouldn't know to protect ourselves.

Anxiety

Anxiety is a feeling like fear. When we are anxious we have bad thoughts.

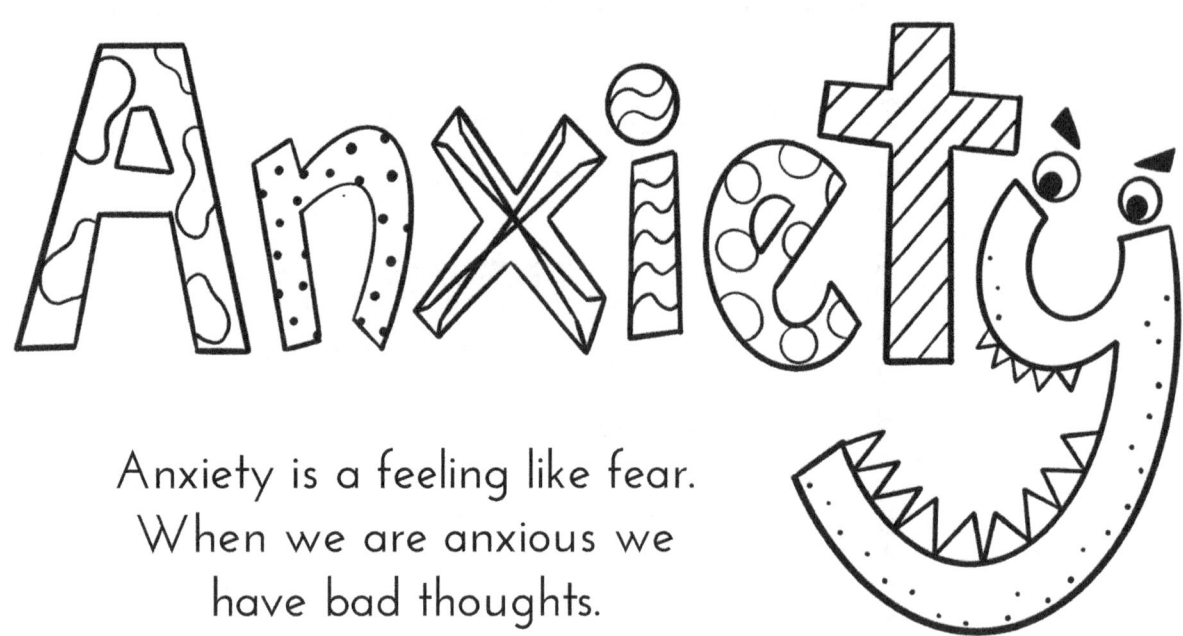

What if?

What if?

What if my parents get divorced?

What if Grandma dies?

What if there is a tornado?

What if I fail the test?

What if?

What if??

Have you ever had a nagging feeling that wouldn't go away? Or a thought that repeated, like an annoying fly buzzing in your ear? These feelings are known as anxiety.

It can catch us at the worst moments. And it can make it difficult to concentrate on other things we should be thinking about. Sometimes it feels like there is no way to escape it.

Can you think of a time that you were anxious?

_____

_____

_____

_____

_____

_____

The thoughts we have create feelings.

When we think of happy things, we feel happier. And when we think of sad things, we feel sadder.

Anxiety is a feeling we have when we think bad things might happen. Or, when we just don't know what will happen.

Draw a picture of a thought that makes you smile.

YOUR MIND IS A GARDEN

If you want to feel happy and worry free, you must first plant the right kinds of thoughts in your head.

POSITIVE THOUGHTS

Your mind can get tricked into believing the things that it hears over and over again - even when those things aren't true! If we keep thinking negative thoughts, we may start to believe them.

Sometimes it helps to say positive things. When we repeat positive thoughts, we trick our brain into thinking a better way. We call these positive thoughts

~ *affirmations* ~

~Rewire~ YOUR BRAIN

When you realize your brain is thinking a bad thought, try replacing it with a better message.

POSITIVE THOUGHTS   NEGATIVE THOUGHTS

Practice saying affirmations out loud or writing them down. Make sure to think of all the reasons why that affirmation is true. A good place to start is to find a negative thought you find yourself thinking or saying a lot. For example:

Instead of saying:
I'm going to fail the math test.

Try saying:
With practice, I will get better at math.
Even though it may be stressful, I can handle it.
I love to learn. I will study hard. I will not give up.
This is just one test. It is not the end of the world.

What negative thought do you find yourself saying?

_____

_____

What positive affirmations can you replace it with?

_____

_____

_____

_____

If you wouldn't say it to a friend ...don't say it to yourself

Meow!

CHALLENGE THOSE NEGATIVE THOUGHTS

Here are some things to ask yourself:

Is what I am thinking actually true?
Is how I'm thinking making me feel worse?
How can I look at this in a positive way?
What is the WORST thing that could happen?
Is it very likely the worst thing will happen?
Is this situation out of my control? Do I have the ability to change it?
What would a good friend or trusted adult say about it?
What has helped me cope before?

Often, these negative thoughts that cause us anxiety are

Some situations are
IN YOUR CONTROL

- ☑ the things you do
- ☑ things that you say
- ☑ how you treat others
- ☑ what you believe
- ☑ your attitude
- ☑ your behaviour
- ☑ the effort you put out

Other situations are
BEYOND YOUR CONTROL

- ☒ things that others do
- ☒ things that others say
- ☒ how others treat you
- ☒ other people's beliefs
- ☒ other people's attitudes
- ☒ other people's behaviour
- ☒ other people's efforts
- ☒ the past

When you are experiencing anxiety, you must ask yourself,

Is this something I control?

A situation that is in your control, is a situation you CAN CHANGE.

THE ONLY THING YOU CAN CHANGE, IS <u>YOU</u>.

It's all about

CHOICES

You may not always be able to choose what happens to you, but you can choose how you respond.

You can't control everything about your future, but you can control a lot of it.

PILOT YOUR LIFE IN THE RIGHT DIRECTION

What if a situation is out of your control?

A situation that is out of your control, is a situation you CANNOT change.

There are many things that we can't control. We can't control where we were born, or the color of our skin. We can't control the weather, or wars that happen, or if people get sick.

Those things are NOT OUR CHOICE.

There is no sense worrying about things beyond your control, because you cannot change those situations. Worrying only makes their impact on us worse.

List 3 things that are IN your control.

_____

_____

_____

List 3 things that are OUT of your control.

_____

_____

_____

WORRY ROBS US OF OUR HAPPINESS

Draw a picture of something you could do
if you never worried about doing it.

Would you dance like nobody was watching?
Talk to someone who you feel shy around?
Tell people what you're REALLY thinking?

Anxiety cannot improve a situation. It can only alert us to situations that may need our attention. Feelings of anxiety, stress, worry or fear cause us to respond. How you respond can make the situation worse, or it can make it better.

Natalie's Situation

Natalie has been given a public speaking assignment to work on. She has to write a 3 minute speech, and then say it in front of the whole class. Speaking in front of groups of people make Natalie very nervous.

What are some actions she can take to make her situation better?

_____

_____

_____

What actions would not improve Natalie's situation?

_____

_____

Julian's Story

Julian's family moved because his dad got a new job in a different town. It meant more money, a nicer neighborhood, and other opportunities for their family. Julian was shy and nervous about starting at a new school where he did not know anyone. Julian was afraid he would not make new friends. He felt angry toward his parents for moving.

The day that he started school, Julian kept to himself. He did not speak to anyone unless they spoke to him first.

His stomach felt tight. At lunchtime he could barely eat. His body felt tingly and he found himself sweating, even though it was a cold day. A jumble of thoughts ran through his head...

> What if they don't like me?
> What if I embarrass myself?

A couple of kids said hello to him. But Julian assumed they were only being nice because the teacher told them to - not because they wanted to.

Weeks went by and Julian finally made new friends and was happy at his new school. But it took a long time.

Let's ask ourselves some questions...

Was moving in or out of Julian's control?
- Moving was out of his control. Julian could not decide where he was going to live. That was his parents' decision.

Should Julian have been angry with his parents?
- Most parents consider, very carefully, big decisions like job changes and moving. Julian's parents felt that it was in their family's best interest to make a change. But it is understandable that Julian was upset. And it is normal to have bad feelings once in a while. And it is okay to be angry with a situation that is out of your control... for a while.

What were symptoms of Julian's anxiety?
- Julian had physical symptoms such as a nervous/sore stomach, and his body reacted differently than it normally would have. For example, he was sweating when it was cold.
- Julian also had anxious thoughts about embarrassing himself, and no one liking him.

How did Julian react to the situation?
- Julian let his anxiety get the better of him. He chose not to talk to anyone because he was afraid. He also chose to think the other kids did not want to speak to him without really knowing if that was true or not.

What was the end result?
- In the end, Julian finally made friends, although it took a while. Is it possible he would have made friends sooner if he had made different choices? The answer is yes! Julian let his anxiety get in the way of taking positive action.

HELP!

All of These Awful Feelings

Anxiety can feel different from one person to the next. Your feelings of anxiety might be different from someone else's. Here is a list of things you might be feeling. Check off the ones that you have experienced.

- ☐ butterflies in your tummy, sore stomach or throwing up
- ☐ trembling, shaking, or jittery feeling
- ☐ being wound up or feeling like you might burst
- ☐ feeling nervous, scared or freaked out
- ☐ breathing rapidly, difficulty breathing or tight feeling in your chest
- ☐ feeling like your heart is racing, our pounding
- ☐ feeling grumpy for no reason
- ☐ feeling overwhelmed
- ☐ getting upset and crying too easily
- ☐ trouble falling asleep, getting a good sleep, or sleeping too much
- ☐ having nightmares
- ☐ thinking of bad memories over and over
- ☐ being afraid to be alone or away from your parents/caregivers
- ☐ fearing things that most people don't find scary
- ☐ feeling like something bad might happen, but not knowing what
- ☐ not wanting to be with friends or spend time with loved ones
- ☐ not wanting to do things that you normally think are fun
- ☐ not caring about things that once were important to you
- ☐ not being able to concentrate on things (example: having difficulty getting homework done, or listening when you are supposed to)

☐ add your own: _____

_____

Ideas for Coping

- GO FOR A WALK OR RIDE A BIKE
- SPEND TIME WITH PETS
- LEARN SOMETHING NEW
- COMPLIMENT YOURSELF
- CRY – IT'S OKAY TO LET IT OUT
- PRAY
- BUILD A FORT
- SING
- PLAN A HAPPY EVENT FOR THE FUTURE
- PLAY A GAME
- BUILD SOMETHING
- WRITE OR SAY AFFIRMATIONS
- READ A BOOK
- DO A PUZZLE
- BREATHE SLOWLY AND CALMLY
- MAKE A GIFT FOR SOMEONE
- TALK TO A FRIEND
- MEMORIZE A POEM OR BIT OF WRITING
- PAMPER YOURSELF ...HAVE A BATH DO YOUR NAILS
- DRAW A PICTURE
- COLOR
- PLANT SOMETHING OR START A GARDEN
- LEAVE POSITIVE MESSAGES FOR OTHERS
- WRITE A LETTER

WRITE A SONG OR POEM

CREATE A SHORT MOVIE/VIDEO

GET CRAFTY - MAKE SOMETHING

CREATE A SECRET CODE

LISTEN TO MUSIC

DANCE

WRITE IN DIARY OR JOURNAL

STRETCH

HELP OTHERS

PLAY WITH SLIME OR PLAY-DOH

PICTURE YOURSELF IN A CALM PLACE

CLEAN AND ORGANIZE

KNIT OR CROCHET

TALK TO A TRUSTED ADULT

ASK FOR A HUG

FORGIVE THOSE WHO HAVE WRONGED YOU

FINISH THINGS THAT NEED DOING

COUNT SLOWLY TO 100

SPEND TIME IN NATURE

WATCH A FUNNY MOVIE

TAKE PHOTOS OR CREATE A PHOTO ALBUM

FIND SOMETHING POSITIVE IN YOUR DAY

CREATE A QUOTE BOOK TO KEEP YOUR FAVORITE QUOTES AND SAYINGS

EXERCISE OR PLAY SPORTS

FIND THE EVERYDAY BEAUTY THAT IS ALL AROUND YOU

MAKE A COLLAGE OF THINGS THAT MAKE YOU HAPPY

GET ENOUGH SLEEP

These are

a few of my

favorite

things...

Fill this page with your favorite things. Use pictures, or words... or both!

ANXIOUS HABITS

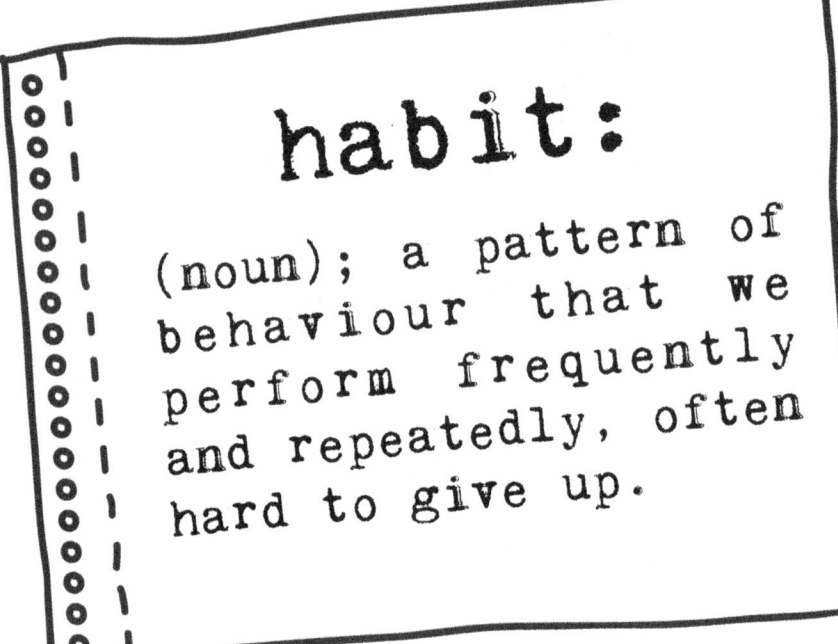

habit:
(noun); a pattern of behaviour that we perform frequently and repeatedly, often hard to give up.

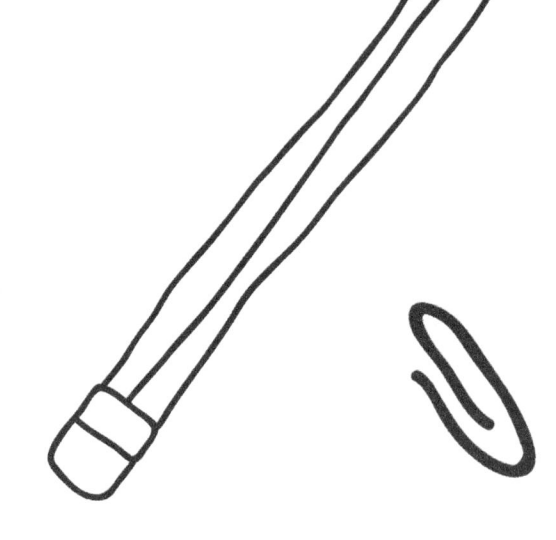

Everyone responds differently to stressful feelings. Sometimes the way we react is through our behaviour. Have you ever found yourself biting your nails, but didn't even realizing you were doing it? Perhaps it felt satisfying at the moment, but later your fingers hurt, and didn't look very nice. And you realize that it would have been better to avoid biting them in the first place.

Let's look at different types of habits that may be caused by anxiety. Do you find yourself doing any of these things? Check off the ones that apply to you.

BODY HABITS
(things that you do to yourself)

- ☐ nail biting
- ☐ toe tapping or knee bouncing
- ☐ skin picking
- ☐ hair twirling or pulling
- ☐ lip or cheek biting

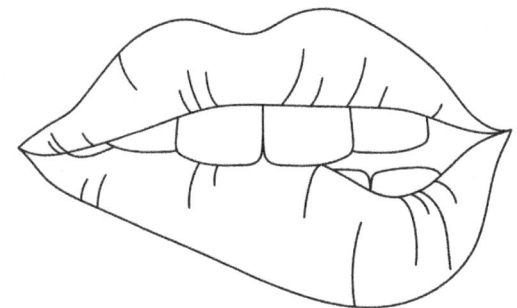

WHAT TO DO ABOUT IT
First, see if you can figure out when and where you find yourself doing it. Do you bounce your knee in class, because you are nervous? Are you picking your skin or pulling hair when you're watching tv or reading? Sometimes, these kinds of habits begin for one reason, like anxiety, but continue for another reason, like boredom. If you can identify the time and place it will happen, you can prevent it.

The easiest way to prevent habits like these are to replace them with better habits. If you skin pick, try keeping your fingers busy doing something else instead, such as knitting, using a fidget spinner, or doodling. Find something enjoyable, that you are more likely to want to continue doing.

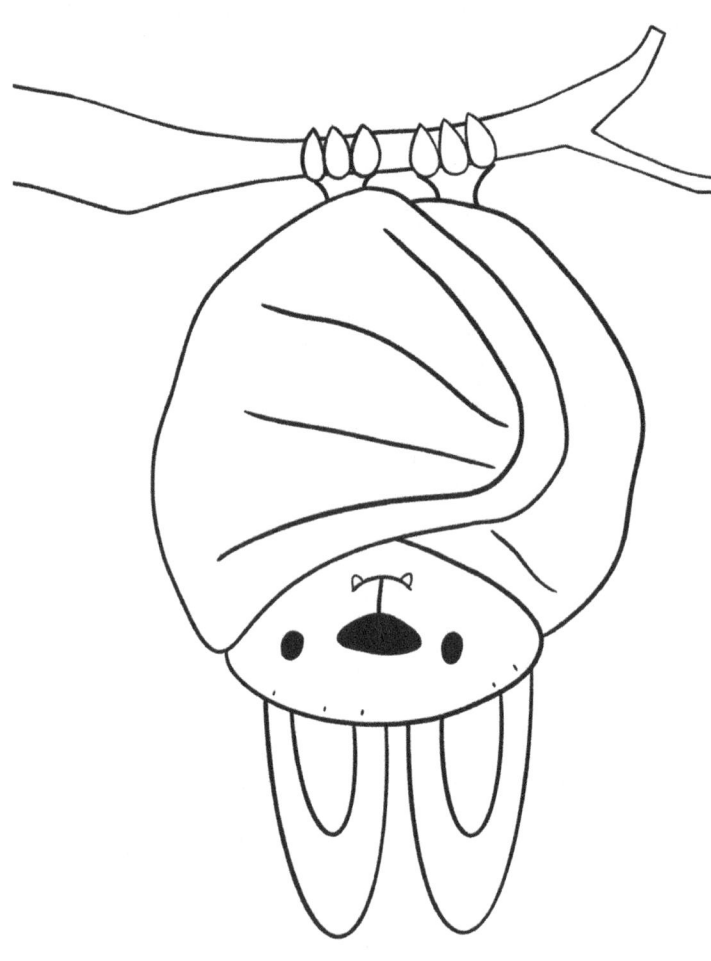

I SLEEP ALL DAY & ALL NIGHT

I GUESS I HAVE BAT HABITS!

Intrusive Thoughts

Intrusive thoughts are ones that pop into our head and make us afraid. They can get stuck in our head and might be difficult to get rid of.

Brittany's Fear of Germs

A couple of years ago, Brittany learned about germs, and how some of them cause illness. Ever since, she has been careful to avoid germs as much as possible. She coughs into her arm, does not share drinks, washes her hands after using the toilet and before eating, and keeps her room spotlessly clean.

Lately, Brittany has been thinking a lot more about germs, and how they could be lurking anywhere. At first, she made sure to do a better job cleaning and washing her hands. Over time, however, she found herself washing things repeatedly… far more than anyone else, even adults. She has become so afraid of germs that she wears gloves to avoid touching any. She does not like to go to public places because of all the germs she could encounter, and she avoids hanging out with her friends now. Brittany can't seem to get rid of the bad thoughts.

Brittany's feelings warned her about the danger of germs. But her brain got stuck in a loop, repeating the warning over and over again. Even when there really wasn't any imminent danger.

Just like Brittany, people who have intrusive thoughts sometimes react by repeating behaviours - like hand washing. And they don't always make sense. Have you ever played the game where you tried not to step on the cracks in the sidewalk… **"Step on a crack, break your mother's back?"** Nobody actually believes that stepping on a crack will hurt anyone. The way we react to intrusive thoughts may not make any sense to others. They may not even make sense to us.

Do you repeat any of these behaviours? Check the ones that apply to you. Then keep reading to find out what to do about them.

- ☐ hand washing
- ☐ turning lights on and off
- ☐ opening and closing doors repeatedly
- ☐ checking and rechecking that things are safe (like locking doors or making sure the stove is turned off)
- ☐ checking or rechecking that people are safe
- ☐ paying too close attention to details
- ☐ feeling the need to memorize things
- ☐ needing everything to be perfect, or laid out in a particular way
- ☐ not being able to throw things out, or keeping trash

Do you ever spend too much time…

- ☐ counting or doing things a certain number of times
- ☐ needing to touch objects
- ☐ rearranging things until they are perfect
- ☐ repeating words or thoughts

THE SCARIEST MONSTERS ARE THE ONES IN YOUR HEAD

Washing your hands a lot, counting, or being very neat about things might not seem like a big deal to those who haven't experienced it. But for the person it is happening to, and the people close to them, it can have a negative effect. The behaviours get in the way of life, and having fun. They create even more anxiety.

The next time you have intrusive thoughts, doubts, and anxiety, please remember...

FEAR IS A LIAR

You do NOT have to be a slave to your fears. You can face them. No matter how scary they seem, or how stressed out you feel about them... they are JUST FEELINGS.

And feelings cannot hurt you, unless you let them.

You are much braver than you think.

It's not just firefighters, and superheroes, and knights in armor that are brave. Anyone can be brave. Even you.

You see, bravery is not being unafraid.
Bravery is having the courage to act even though you are afraid.

Fear is a bully. It taunts you, and tells you all sorts of bad things about yourself. Things that aren't even true. It makes you feel weak. So we must treat fear the same way we treat bullies... You have to stand up to it! You have to let it know that you won't believe it's lies. And that no matter what it does, you will not let it change you.

Draw yourself fighting your fear monster.

YOU MAY FEEL LIKE A kitten BUT YOU HAVE THE HEART OF A lion

Find yourself a cheerleader

Before you begin to tackle your fears all by yourself... I want you to find yourself a cheerleader. A cheerleader is on TEAM YOU. Cheerleaders are people who want what is best for you and will stick with you through your hard times. They are there to cheer you on and encourage you.

If you have fear, or anxiety, you should **TELL SOMEONE** about it. It is nothing to be ashamed of. Everyone has fears from time to time. Everyone experiences anxiety now and then. If they say they don't, they might just be too embarrassed to tell you about it. Or they are trying to fix it all by themselves. And that is never a good idea.

Everyone needs a support system. The first place you should look for support is within your family. But if you feel like you can't talk to them, find an adult you trust, perhaps a teacher, pastor or school counsellor. You can also turn to friends who are honest and trustworthy, and who make good decisions. If you really feel like there is nobody around who you can talk to, you can find **free phone numbers** to speak with someone who will listen at back of this book.

Sometimes our fears make us feel different from other people. And we feel like nobody will care or understand. But that's simply not true. You're not weird, or different. Many people have experienced what you are going through. Most people just don't talk about it much.

WHO IS YOUR HERO?

We all need people to look up to. Heroes come in all shapes and sizes. They can be our next door neighbors, historical figures, someone you've seen on tv... anyone really. Who do you admire? Can you think of someone who has done something brave?

NAME: _____

HOW THEY WERE BRAVE: _____

_____
_____
_____
_____
_____
_____
_____
_____
_____

I've goat a good feeling about this!

So... you've got your cheerleader by your side, you've got someone to look up to, and you're trying really hard to be brave. Check, check... and check. Now you are ready to tackle those fears like a boss! Time to show 'em you're no pussy cat... you're a lion... or a ferocious fear-eating goat... Rooooaaaar! Baaaa!

Facing Your Fears

The best way to conquer a fear is to face it.
You were born to be a happy, confident person.
You can't let fear change that. You must fight back.

Now, I know we've talked about being roaring goat lions... and you can roar out loud if it helps (try it!). But facing your fear is often a quiet thing that happens in your mind. Here is what we suggest:

First...

- Close your eyes.
- Focus on your breathing.
- Breathe in and out, very slowly. In 1-2-3-4. And out 1-2-3-4.
- Can you feel your heart rate slowing? Good.

Second...
- Think of the thing that scares you.
- Remember... these bad thoughts cannot hurt you. They are just thoughts.
- Some people like to pray for help and guidance.

Third...
- Imagine yourself conquering your fear and being okay. Picture yourself handling the situation, and getting through it.

PHOBIAS

Phobias are fears that cause us to overreact to threats (or things our mind tells us are threats). Brittany's fear of germs is an example of a phobia. Some other common ones are fear of spiders, flying in airplanes, heights, thunderstorms, elevators, snakes... There are many.

Ryker and the Mouse

Ten year old Ryker's classmates discovered that he was afraid of mice. So they decided to play a prank on him. One of them screamed, "A mouse!" and pointed under Ryker's desk.

Ryker panicked. First, he screamed. Then crawled up on top of the desk. He was so scared, he cried. Ryker's classmates laughed. Do you think Ryker overreacted?

If Ryker had remained calm, he might have been able to tell that the other kids were fooling him. And if he really thought about it, a tiny little mouse should be far more scared of people, than people should be of a mouse.

Is a mouse a real threat? Could it hurt him? Possibly. It could bite. And it might be carrying germs that could make him sick. But still, a two inch long mouse is no immediate threat to a ten year old boy.

Aaaack! Run for your lives! The HUMANS are coming!

How to Fix a Phobia

If you have a phobia that you want to get rid of, there is a ~~very easy~~ way to do so. You simply have to expose yourself to thing that you fear. Just a little bit at a time, of course.

Ryker wanted to get over his fear of mice. So he put himself in situations where he could experience them. His fear was pretty bad, so he decided to start off slow. This is how Ryker did it:

DAY 1: Ryker went to the library and read books about mice. He learned what they eat, and about their behaviour. He looked at pictures of them. At first they are hard to look at, but as he learned more and more, they didn't seem quite so bad. They were a even a bit interesting.

DAY 2: Ryker went to his local pet store. He watched mice in cages from far away. Ryker was brave, though, and managed to get a few steps closer.

DAY 3-4: Ryker returned to the pet store two more times. By the end of his thrid visit, he was able to get close to the glass cage, and touch it. He sees the mouse behaviours he read about, up close.

DAY 5: Ryker fed a mouse. He practiced his breathing first, and remained calm. The mouse took a sunflower seed right out of his hand. Ryker worked up enough courage to touch the mouse. He was no longer feaful, only a bit nervous. After a few seeds, Ryker let the mouse crawl on his hand. The experience isn't as bad as thought it would be. It's actually kind of fun!

6 MONTHS LATER... Ryker's parents let him have a pet mouse. He named him Cheddar. Ryker barely remembers why he was scared in the first place.

THE GAME PLAN

Lets make a plan to tackle your fear monster. Start by filling in the blanks.

WHAT ARE YOU AFRAID OF?

_____

_____

WHO CAN YOU LOOK UP TO?

_____

WHO IS YOUR CHEERLEADER?

_____

WRITE DOWN ONE OR TWO AFFIRMATIONS TO HELP YOU.

_____

_____

_____

STEP 1:

STEP 2:

STEP 3:

STEP 4:

REACH FOR THE STARS

TURN YOUR GOALS INTO PLANS

PICTURE IT IN YOUR MIND

Close your eyes and think of how you will react the next time you are in an anxious situation. Think it through, from beginning to happy ending, like a movie. Then write/draw it, in the space below.

TAKING CARE OF YOURSELF

If we want to become champion fear fighters, our bodies and minds need to be in good shape. We need to take care of ourselves. But if our thoughts are preoccupied with bad thoughts, we might forget.

Did you know that exercise, nutrition, and sleep affect the way your brain works?

EXERCISE releases chemicals called endorphins that make us feel good. They help us sleep better and improve brain function.

GOOD NUTRITION is not just fuel for your body. It is also fuel for your brain. Stress zaps us of energy, but eating well keeps us energized. It also helps us to think more clearly. Negative feelings makes some of us want to eat too much, too little, or make bad food choices. But those things only make us feel worse. Life is hard when you have stress. It's even harder if you have stress *and* indigestion.

GETTING A GOOD SLEEP and getting enough sleep reduces stress. Sleeping gives our brain a break from stress. It helps us to think more clearly.

TAKE CARE OF YOURSELF THE WAY YOU WOULD TAKE CARE OF SOMEONE YOU LOVE

EXERCISE

Kids need at least one hour of exercise per day... the kind of exercise that **gets your heart pumping** and makes you **breathe faster**. It doesn't matter what you do, whether it's playing hockey, riding your bike, jumping on a trampoline, dancing, jogging with your dog, or swimming. It all counts, so long as it does those two things.

What is your favorite way to get your body moving? Draw a picture.

Exercise Tracker

Small habits can have big results! Color in a square every time you have exercised for a whole hour. See how long it takes you.

START DATE:..................................

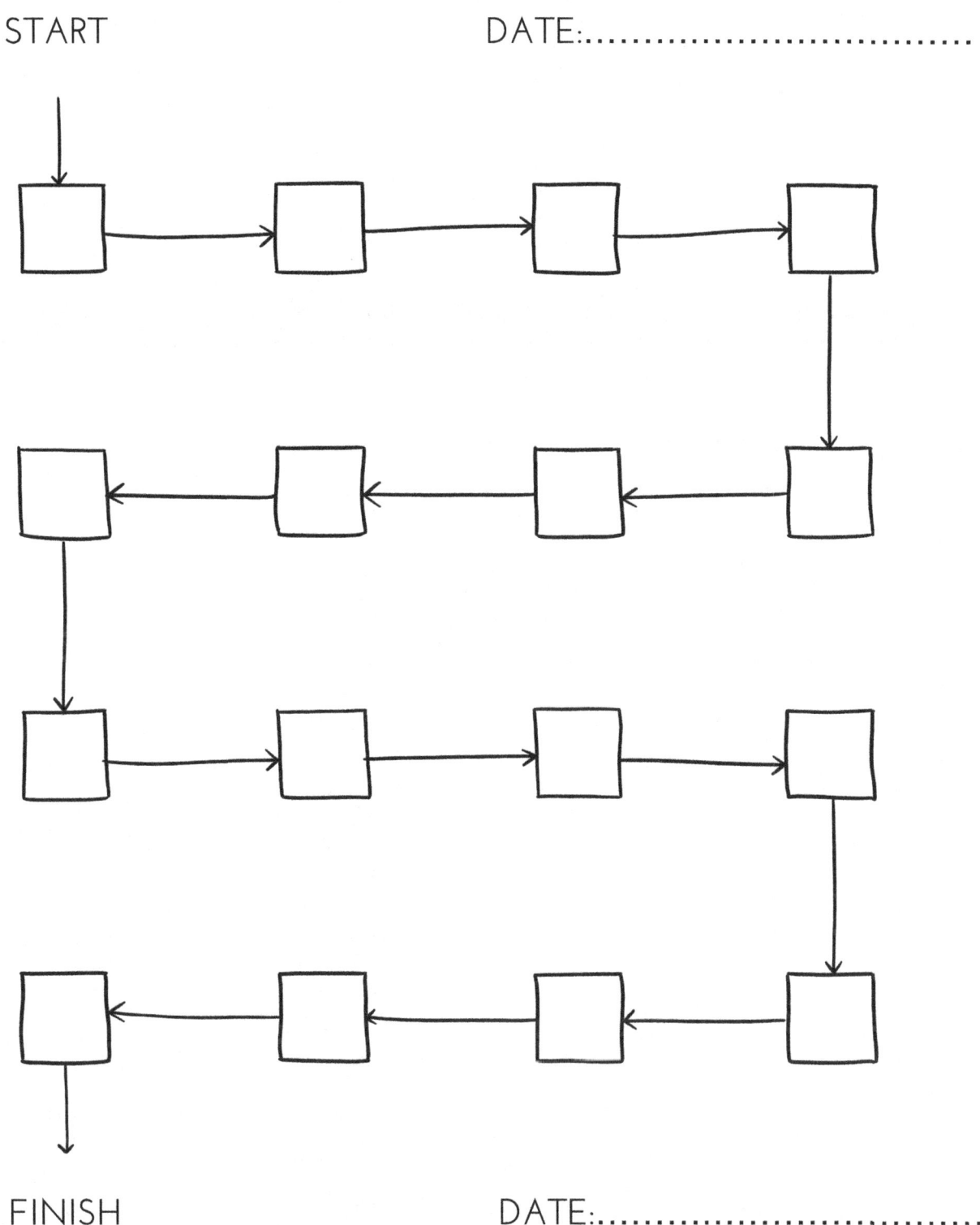

FINISH DATE:..................................

We all know that eating the right foods, and amounts of food are important for our brains and our bodies to be healthy. That means we should be eating a diet of vegetables, whole grains and proteins. Ideally, we should be eating those foods in the form of 3 meals, plus 1 or 2 snacks per day.

nom nom nom nom nom

Have you ever heard the expression, "You are what you eat?" If that was true, what kind of food would you be?

A PICTURE OF ME AS THE FOOD I EAT THE MOST

I MAKE GOOD CHOICES

Let's see how many different GOOD FOOD choices you can make. Fill in each ray of the sun with your good food choice. it can be the type of food, the amount of food, or choosing to not eat an unhealthy food. You may also color in the rays as you go.

HOW TO GET A GOOD NIGHT'S REST

Is anxiety keeping you up at night? Kids between the ages of six and ten need about 10-11 hours of sleep per night. That sleep should happen all at once. Follow these steps to get a good sleep:

STEP 1: Get stuff done. This should happen during the day, or early evening, long before you go to sleep. We all have responsibilities - chores, homework, tests to study for, etc. When we wait too long, we can find ourselves scrambling to finish these tasks when we should be relaxing or sleeping. Worse, if we don't complete them at all, they add to our stress and anxiety.

STEP 2: Relax and unwind for an hour or two before bed. This is not the time to be exercising, eating, or doing any of the things mentioned in step 1.

STEP 3: Have a routine. That means going to bed at the same time every night, and waking up at the same time every morning. Spend a few minutes doing the same things every night before you go to bed, such as brushing your teeth, washing your face, and putting on your pajamas. Routines help our bodies to develop rythms. Your body will come to know when it is time to sleep and time to wake up.

STEP 4: Comfy clothes and no distractions. It's just not comfortable to wear shoes or tight-fitting clothing to bed. And nobody wants to be woken up in the middle of the night because they are sleeping on toys or books, or because their phone buzzed.

STEP 5: Set an alarm. Put it across the room so you are not tempted to press the snooze button when it goes off in the morning. This will help your body get into a routine. And try not to sleep in more than an hour on weekends. That will throw your body's routine off. Plus, you can accomplish so much more, when you wake up early, get dressed and start your day.

Sleep Tracker

How many hours of sleep do you get a night? Color in one sheep for every hour you slept. Remember, you should be aiming for between 10-11 ~~sheep~~ hours per night.

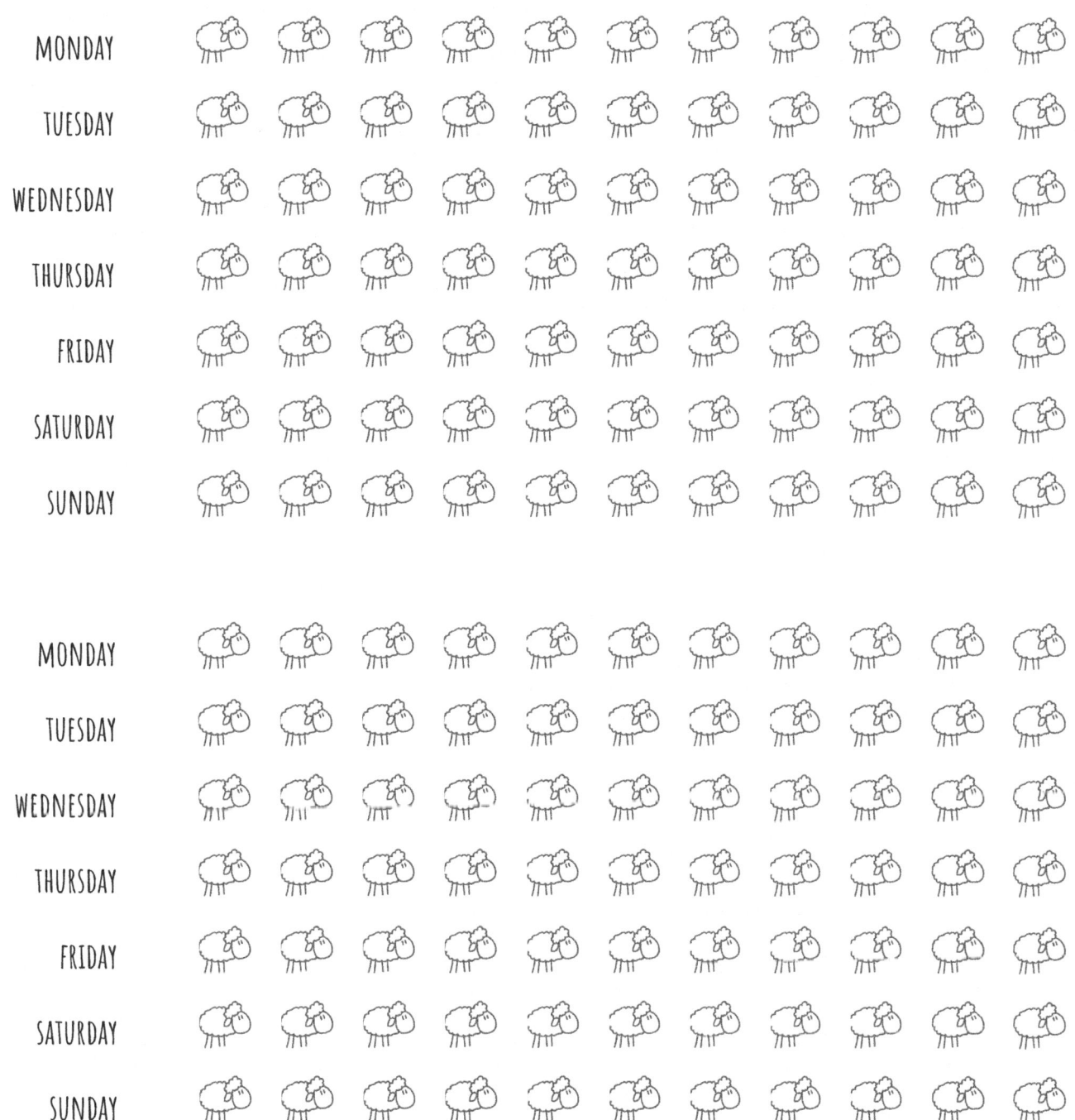

NIGHTMARES

Being anxious also cause us to have bad dreams. And bad dreams can cause us to be anxious. Falling asleep is hard to do when you think you're going to have a nightmare. The important thing to remember is that...

Bad dreams are just thoughts... and thoughts cannot hurt you!

Dreams may be your brain's way of sorting through your day, working out problems, or learning while you sleep. Sometimes we might wonder how our brains can produce such strange, unwanted thoughts while we are asleep. Even scientists do not have all the answers as to why we dream the things we do.

The impotant thing to remember is that you cannot think things into existence. Just because you dream something, does not mean it will come true.

Instead of being scared to fall asleep, think about your favorite things next time... a fun experience, a funny story, or things you really like, whether it's baseball, roller coasters, or unicorns. Happy thoughts make for happier dreams.

I'M SO GOOD AT SLEEPING, I CAN DO IT WITH MY EYES CLOSED

Sophie's Busy Week

Sophie loves to help other people. At school, she volunteers to help put away library books during lunchtime, paints backdrops for the play, and regularly helps with the school's recycling. Sophie has a very busy schedule. On Mondays and Wednesdays, she looks after her neighbor's kids until their mother gets home from work. On Tuesdays she has broomball. On Thursdays she delivers flyers. And Friday nights she attends dance class. Weekends are busy, too, with cleaning, shopping and visiting relatives.

Sophie is so busy she doesn't have much time to spend with friends or just relax. Lately she feels anxious and unhappy a lot of the time. She just doesn't care about anything as much as she used to. And her grades have dropped.

The thing that Sophie lacks in her life is...

balance.

Balance is being able to make time for everything in your life, in a way that you can manage them all, and be happy.

Sophie is participating in so many activities that she doesn't have time for things that make her happy, like friends. And she doesn't have time to focus on other things that matter, like schoolwork.

Having a balanced life means having time for both work and play. If all you ever did all day was schoolwork, you wouldn't have time for other things. And if all you did was play, and didn't study, your grades would suffer. We also need the right balance of sleep to being awake, and healthy food choices to unhealthy treats. When our bodies and lives are in balance, we are healthier and happier.

FINDING THE RIGHT BALANCE WILL KEEP YOU FROM FALLING

BE CAREFUL HOOOO

YOU LISTEN TOOOO!

The people we are surrounded by have an enormous effect on our emotions. Think about how you feel when you are with people who are happy and laughing and having a good time. Do you feel differently than when you are with people who are negative, angry and sad?

There are times when it is appropriate to be angry or sad just as there are times when it is appropriate to be happy and joyful. You probably wouldn't laugh and joke around at a funeral. Just like you probably wouldn't cry, complain, and make angry remarks at a birthday party.

NEGATIVE NELLIES

Have you ever known someone who got stuck in a negative state? They are the kind of people who rarely seem to be happy and complain all the time, even when things aren't that bad. The kind of people who always see the downside of a situation. They rarely ever have anything nice to say. Negative Nellies tend to spread their misery to anyone who will listen.

We must be careful who we spend time with. Just like germs, our emotions and attitudes are contagious. Spending too much time with Negative Nellies can cause you to come down with a bad case of

negative-itis

POSITIVE vibes only

You can be a good, caring, helpful friend to someone with a problem - without adopting their attitude. But...

you are not responsible for anyone else's happiness

The only time you are responsible for someone else's feelings is if you hurt or wronged them. If that is the case, you need to apologize and try not to do it again. Just remember, you are NOT IN CONTROL of what other people think or feel, or the choices they make.

Happiness isn't something that happens only to lucky people. If that were the case, it would be difficult to find happy people who are poor or disabled. And that is just not so. A large part of happiness depends on the choices you make, and the attitude you have.

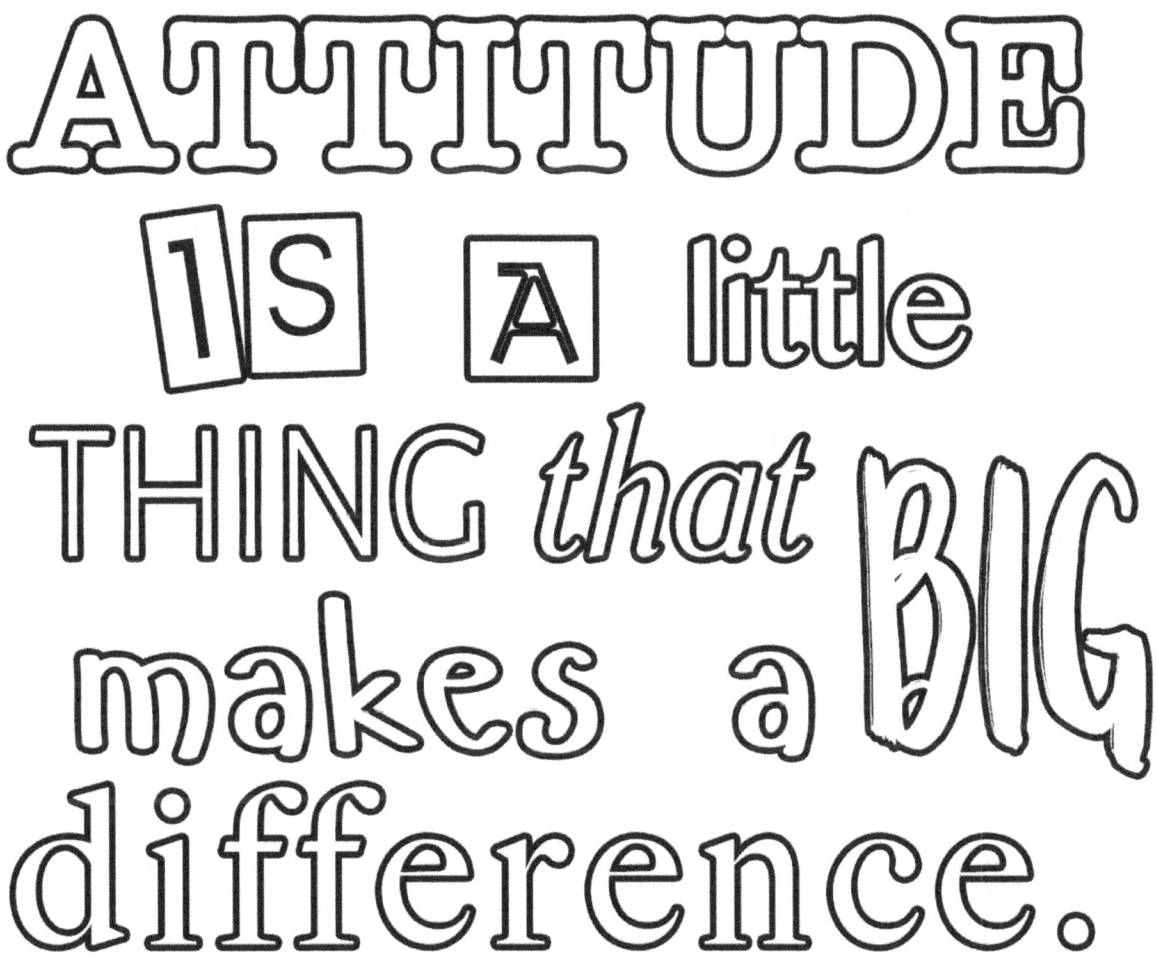

ATTITUDE IS A little THING that makes a BIG difference.

POSITIVE PALS

Make a list of five positive people you know. What special quality do each of them has that makes you like being around them.

NAME	SPECIAL QUALITY
1.	QUALITY:
2.	QUALITY:
3.	QUALITY:
4.	QUALITY:
5.	QUALITY:

WHEN SOMEONE MAKES YOU ANXIOUS

We can't always avoid people who make us anxious. Perhaps they are a parent, or the person who sits next to you in school. Though we may not be able to control what they say to us, we can control how we react. Here are some ideas you can use:

1. Ask Them to Stop: Tell them they are making you uncomfortable. This can be difficult to do without offending someone. Try saying,

"I'd rather not talk/think about that."
or… "I prefer to look at the bright side of things."

2. Ignore Them: Make it clear, without being rude, that you are not interested in what they have to say. This means to give as little reaction as possible to what their words.

"Mice are going to take over the world someday."

"I heard the pond safety test is really hard. I bet we're gonna fail."

"Hey… why are you wearing THAT shade of green?"

"I knew this tadpole once who went through the exact same thing you're going through. He got eaten by a fish."

"Hmmmm."

PUT IT DOWN ON PAPER

It can be easier to write our thoughts down on paper, instead of remembering what we wanted to say in the moment. It gives us time to choose just the right words to express our feelings. If you are having trouble saying the right thing in a situation, try writing it down.

Write a letter to the person who makes you anxious. Let them know how the things they say affect you. Be aware of the reader's feelings, too. Try adding something positive into your letter at the beginning and end.

Here is an example:

Dear Toad,

I really enjoy hanging out at the lily pad and catching flies with you. But lately, some of the things we talk about have made me feel bad. Hearing about the mice, the test, and that missing tadpole are kinda stressing me out. I like it better when we talk about fly fishing and make worm jokes. I'm telling you this because you have always been a good friend and I knew you would understand.

Your pal,

Frog

PS: Your worm jokes are the best!

Now it's your turn. What would you like to say to the person who is stressing you out? Use this page as a test copy or to write down your ideas.

Even if you don't send it, it can be helpful to put your thoughts down on paper.

Dear _____

PROTECTING YOURSELF

You may not be able to explain your anxiety to others in a way that they will get it. True friends, and the people will love you will want to understand or help. Some people might be too caught up in their own problems. And then there are those that will try to cause you anxiety on purpose. Those people are <u>bullies</u>. Bullies like to hurt others because they are hurting also. They want to make everyone feel as miserable as they do. Bullies are not the sort of people we should keep close to us.

In medieval times, thick, tall walls were built around castles and sometimes their towns. Walls kept out enemies and kept the people inside them safe. If you wanted to enter the castle, you had to go through a gate. You needed permission to enter. We too should be choosy about who we let in.

Like medieval castles, it is sometimes necessary to seperate ourselves from those who would hurt us. And that is okay. You do not need to be friends with everyone. It is normal and healthy to want to avoid people like that. If you cannot avoid a bully, you may need to stand up to them. Because if you let someone treat you badly, they will usually keep right on doing it.

WHAT TO DO:
- Remain calm. Do not be emotional.
- Do not shrink back or turn away. Look them right in the eye.
- Tell them to STOP, loudly and clearly, so they and others hear.
- Use few words. Do not get into a conversation.
- Get help from a teacher, parent or trusted adult. This is not tattling.
- At school, ask to be moved to a different seat/locker.

Remember to always be respectful. And always treat others the way you would like to be treated, even when they don't do the same.

I UNDERSTAND IF YOU DON'T LIKE ME... NOT EVERYONE HAS GOOD TASTE.

Our own words and actions play an important role in how we feel about ourselves. It is easy to put the blame on others when we feel bad. And difficult to see our own faults and shortcomings.

Nobody is perfect.

It's a fact... you are going to mess up sometimes (some of us mess up more than others). And you know what? That's okay. Making mistakes is one of the ways we learn.

WHAT TO DO WHEN YOU MAKE A MISTAKE

Mistakes can make us feel like we are not good enough. They cause us to worry how others will think and react. They can be embarrassing.

There are 2 kinds of mistakes:

HONEST MISTAKES

Honest mistakes are the kind that you didn't know you could prevent. Like when you get the wrong answer on a test, because you were sick the day you talked about it in class. or when you form an idea about something, without knowing all the details.

Lena's Honest Mistake

Lena assumed that her neighbor, Mrs. Cortez, liked wearing wigs and changing her hairstyle. "I like your new wig, Mrs, Cortez," Lena said one day, "but I prefer your natural hair better." Soon after, Lena came to find out that Mrs. Cortez had cancer and had lost all of her hair due to the medications she was taking to fight it. This was why she had been wearing wigs. Lena felt awful about what she had said.

Lena did not mean to be insensitive. She just didn't have all the facts. She never wanted to hurt Mrs. Cortez's feelings. Had she known, she never would have made such a comment. Her mistake was an accident.

Honest mistakes are nothing to be ashamed of. They happen to everyone from time to time. Nobody should make you feel bad for not knowing something, because none of us know everything.

YOU DON'T KNOW WHAT YOU DON'T KNOW.

BAD DECISIONS

We use the word mistake a lot, meaning an honest mistake. But many times we call things mistakes that aren't. These kinds of mistakes are things that should be called bad decisions. To help you understand the difference, a bad decision is when...

- I knew better but I did it anyway.

- I did something wrong and feel bad about it now.

- I did something wrong, then got caught, and now I'm pretending that it was honest mistake, but really I'm just lying.

Corben and Mr. Wiggles

Corben's class has a pet hamster named Mr. Wiggles. Each child gets a turn for one week to care for him. They must feed him and keep his cage clean. The rules are that nobody can pick Mr. Wiggles up or take him out of his cage except for the person looking after him. And only with an adult present.

Corben really wanted to hold Mr. Wiggles, but it was not his week and he was impatient. Instead, it was Erin's turn to look after the hamster. Corben begged Erin, "Please, can I hold him? Just one time!"

But Erin followed the rules and said, "No. You have to wait your turn." Then Erin took Mr. Wiggles' water bottle and went down the hall to fill it up, leaving Corben alone in the classroom with the animal.

While, she was gone, Corben decided that he could hold the hamster, and Erin would never know. Just for a few seconds, then he would put him right back. So he opened the cage door, stuck his hand inside, and scooped the tiny creature up.

Mr Wiggles was very soft and his little nose never stopped moving. Wouldn't it be fun, thought Corben, if Mr Wiggles could crawl on me? I bet he would fit in my shirt pocket. So he took the hamster out of the cage, and put him against his chest.

He was just getting Mr. Wiggles to explore his pocket when he heard footsteps coming. In a hurry, he picked the hamster up out of his pocket. But Mr. Wiggles, wiggled free… and fell to the floor with a plop and a lot of very loud squeaking. And his tiny leg dragged behind him a little.

Horrified, Corben tried to pick the hamster up off the floor, and put him back in his cage but the poor little thing screeched and bit him very hard. Corben screeched too.

It was at that moment, that Erin walked back in, along with the teacher.

"I didn't mean too. It was a mistake!" Corben blurted out.

Corben did three things wrong. Do you know what they were?

1. _____
   _____

2. _____
   _____

3. _____
   _____

Were Corben's choices…

☐ Innocent Mistakes or
☐ Bad Decisions

Mr. Wiggles ended up having a broken leg. The teacher brought him to a veterinarian to have x-rays taken and to have the bone set. He was also prescribed medicine for the pain.

What can Corben do to show responsibility for his wrongdoings?

_____
_____
_____
_____

You are responsible for how you act... no matter how you feel.

RESPONSIBILITY

We are responsible for the choices we make, whether they are good decisions or bad decisions. Sometimes it seems easier to make a bad decision because of how we feel. But bad decisions have bad consequences.

For example…

- You might not feel like studying for a test… but then you might fail.

- You might feel like saying something mean to a friend who is annoying you… but they might decide not to be your friend anymore.

- You might not feel like saving your money, because you would like to spend it all right away… but then you will not get the thing that you were saving for.

We don't always get everything we want. And it is okay to be disappointed when you don't get your way. Being disappointed for a short time is much better than dealing with the consequences of bad decisions.

When was a time when you made a bad decision? What was the consequence?

_____

_____

_____

_____

What Corben Did Wrong...

Corben <u>really</u> wanted to hold Mr. Wiggles, even though he knew it was against the rules. And he made some bad decisions, didn't he?

- First, he tried to convince Erin to break the rules.
- Next, he took the hamster out of the cage.
- Then, instead of admitting his wrongdoing and apologizing, Corben said it was a mistake - as if it were not somehow his own fault. But it was not an honest mistake. He knew he was breaking the rules and did it anyway, because of how he felt.

Dropping Mr. Wiggles was an accident. Corben never meant for that to happen. But dropping Mr. Wiggles <u>only happened</u> because Corben broke the rules, so Corben is still responsible.

In the end, Corben admitted his wrongdoings and he apologized. Corben used all of the money in his piggy bank to pay for the hamster's vet bills. And Corben learned a valuable lesson... that being disappointed for a short time, was better than breaking the rules and dealing with the consequences later.

WHAT DOES ANY OF THIS HAVE TO DO WITH ANXIETY?

Dealing with the consequences of bad decisions is stressful! Making bad choices gives us anxiety in three ways:

1. We feel bad or guilty about the choice we make.
2. Then we find ourselves worrying about getting caught, and having to deal with the consequences later.
3. Bad decisions result in bad consequences. Sometimes those consequences affect others. They disappoint the people who love us, and can sometimes hurt others, even if we did not intend for anyone to get hurt.

THINK ABOUT THE CONSEQUENCES before you act.

If I do this... what might happen?

Integrity

DO THE RIGHT THING EVEN WHEN NO ONE IS LOOKING

If you want to have less to worry about... simply do what is right. Can you think of a time when you did something you shouldn't have and worried about getting caught? We all make mistakes and bad choices. but when we do what feels good in the moment instead of doing the right thing, we pay for it later. That causes us anxiety and makes us feel bad about ourselves, and bad for those we may have hurt, too.

You might have a lot of integrity, and it may have nothing to do with why you are anxious. But it still helps. It makes you a person who can be trusted and counted on. Everyone respects people like that. Having integrity gives us peace of mind, because we did the right thing and made good choices.

Can you think of someone who has a lot of integrity? Who are they, and why?

_____

_____

_____

_____

_____

Not everyone has integrity or plays by the rules. And no matter how hard you try to do the right thing, there will always be others that won't. They may lie, cheat and steal from us. They might hurt our feelings, or worse.

more about BULLIES

Bullies are people who:

- Hurt you by hitting, kicking, punching, slapping, etc.
- Call you names, insults you, and make you feel bad by what they say.
- Spread rumors about you or make others not like you.
- Harrass you online through texting, social media, and emails.
- Pretend to be your friend, but don't actually want you to be happy.

The most important thing to know, is that if someone is hurting you… and you are unable to defend yourself or stand up to them, you should tell a trusted adult. Talk to your parents, or a teacher, or someone who can help. You do not deserve to be bullied.

Bullying is wrong, and needs to be stopped.

Hurt Feelings

It's not just bullies who hurt our feelings. Friends, family, and sometimes strangers can do that too. Everyone has moments when they slip up and act like a jerk. Just like you, they are not perfect either. And we have to expect that others will have bad days, or times when they lash out in anger or frustration.

Have you heard of the golden rule? It says...

Do unto others as you would have them do unto you.

That means, you should treat others the way that you want to be treated. It is about respecting others, and seeing that they have value and worth, just like you do.

You already know it is wrong to hurt others on purpose. But did you know it is also wrong to get people back after they hurt you? This is why we have rules and laws. Rules and laws set consequences for wrongdoings. If a thief were to break into your home and steal from you, you would call the police and the thief would go to jail. If you decided, instead, to find the thief's home, and break in, and rob him back, it would be wrong. Because stealing is wrong, even if you steal from a thief. And you would would face the same punishment.

You don't fix a wrongdoing, by doing wrong yourself. Or perhaps you have heard it said, **two wrongs don't make a right**.

What happens when you payback someone who has wronged you? They get angry, and want to hurt you back even more. This kind of thinking leads to a ongoing cycle of hurt. The only way to break that cycle is to do the right thing.

Every DAY IS A chance TO GET BETTER!

Jack and Callie

Jack decided to prank his sister, Callie, by putting a toy bug in her sandwich. Later, at school when she bit into it, and saw the bug, she was horrified, and nearly threw up. Everyone in the cafeteria laughed. And when Jack announced, that he had done it, they cheered him on, and told him what a good prank it was. For a long time afterward, kids teased Callie about bugs being in her lunch, and everywhere.

Jack was only having fun. He never meant any harm to his sister. But Callie did not care. She wanted revenge. A few days later, Callie spilled some water in her brother's lap and told everyone he had peed his pants. And this sparked a war between the brother and sister.

Jack put dye in Callie's shampoo that left her pale blonde hair a greyish color for a whole week. In return, Callie poked holes in Jack's bike tires. Neither one of them admitted to their wrongdoings. They spread rumors about each other to their friends. And they tried to get the other in trouble whenever they could. They went from being normal, happy siblings who loved each other, to enemies who were always on guard.

The last prank came when Callie took the class's fundraising money, hid it in her brother's locker and got Jack in trouble. Jack was suspended from school. Their parents were furious, and both kids were grounded for the rest of the school year.

Jack and Callie eventually apologized, and mended their relationship. But it was never the same as it had once been.

Callie let her anger get the best of her. She wanted to make Jack feel as embarrassed as she did. It didn't matter whether he deserved it or not. She made a bad choice because her feelings were hurt.

Then Jack and Callie got into a cycle of wanting to get the other back, and in worse ways. Their pranking got way out of control. And because of this, the consequences were pretty severe. Do you think it was worth it? Did it make either one of them any happier?

The one thing that Callie and Jack did not do was forgive each other.

FORGIVENESS

When somebody does you wrong, you have to make a choice. You can be angry and let that anger stir inside you, or you can forgive. Forgiveness is when you decide to stop being angry and resentful. It does not make the other person's wrongdoing okay. It just means that you have decided not to let their wrongdoing make you want to do wrong in return.

When we practice forgiveness, we show grace.

GRACE

Grace is something you give to others who do not deserve it. Forgiving someone is a kind of grace. Treating others with kindness, even when they have not been kind to us, is grace. To show grace is to treat other people with respect, simply because they are human beings.

Grace is practicing the golden rule - to treat others as you would want to be treated.

But... but... but that's not fair!

If you're thinking that forgiveness and grace don't seem fair, you're right. They don't. But forgiveness and grace aren't about the person who wronged you. They are about **YOU**.

Nobody wants to be a victim. Staying hurt and angry keeps you that way. It makes you want to do the same thing in return. Which just creates more hurt and anger. And it spreads, like a bad cold.

However...

Choosing to forgive and showing grace creates good feelings. It makes us feel stronger - less like a victim. It stops the cycle of wrongdoing and replaces it with a cycle of kindness.

FORGIVE SOMEONE

Write a letter to someone who has hurt you. Don't worry, you don't have to send it to them if you don't want to. Explain how their actions affected you. Let them know the ways you will try to forgive them and why.

Dear _____

_____

_____

_____

_____

_____

_____

_____

_____

_____

_____

Do Good Things

Have you ever been at the window at a drive-thru restaurant, and found out the person ahead of you paid for your order? In 2014 at a Starbucks in Florida, 760 people, in a row, paid for the order of the person after them in line. It took took days before someone broke the cycle.

Random acts of kindness like that feel really good. They focus your attention on others, instead of on yourself and your own problems. When we focus on the things that cause us to worry, it makes us feel worse. Spreading kindness to others, and making their lives a little better or happier, makes us happier, too!

What small ways can you spread kindness around?

_____

_____

_____

_____

_____

_____

_____

_____

MY RANDOM ACTS OF KINDNESS

Your assignment: to go out into the world and spread kindness and joy to others. Every time you do, make a happy face out of one of the circles.

Be Thankful for the Little Things

Have you ever received something that you had been wanting soooo bad? Were you thankful? I imagine you were. But what about the little things that we sometimes take for granted? Like when your Mom makes your favorite supper? Or when you finally find something you had been searching for a long time? And what about even smaller things that we don't always think of? Like the beauty of the changing seasons? Or having a warm bed to sleep in?

When we practice gratitude, we focus on all the good and wonderful things in our life, and not on our anxiety.

Gratitude means to be grateful or thankful.

Being thankful changes how you see the world! You just have to look around to discover all the little things there are to be thankful for. Soon, you will discover things to be grateful for, that you never even thought about before.

A WEEK OF GRATITUDE

Find 3 things to be grateful for every day...

Today I am grateful for...
1
2
3

Today I am grateful for...
1
2
3

Today I am grateful for...
1
2
3

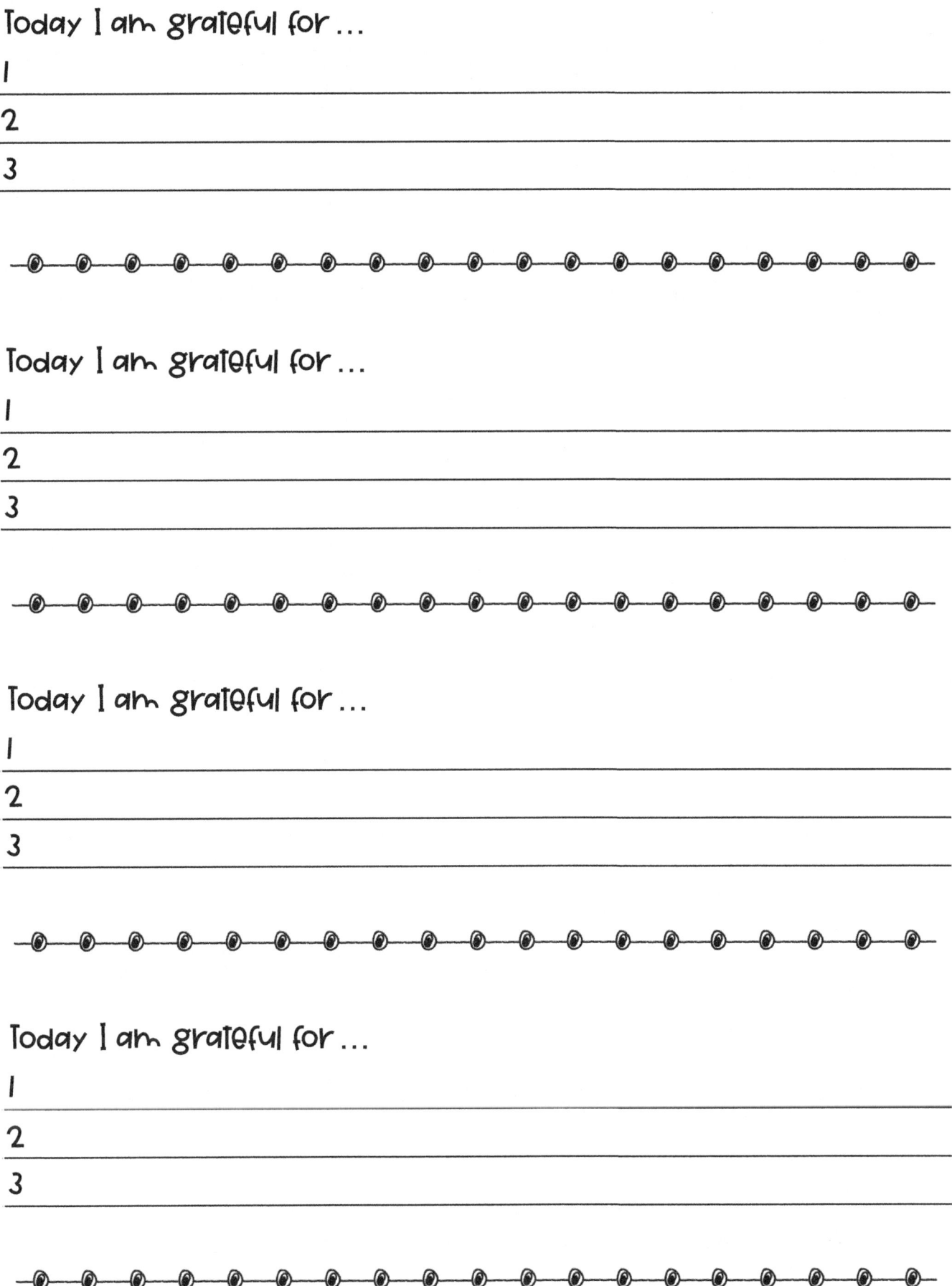

A Higher Power

Many people find comfort in believing in a power higher than themselves - like God, or a Creator. Knowing that there is someone/something out there who is in control of the things is a relief for some of us. It can answer the big questions that people don't have answers for. What do you pray for?

My Prayer

_____
_____
_____
_____
_____
_____
_____
_____
_____
_____
_____

You are not alone

THE PAST IS IN THE PAST

What do you know now, that you wish you had known when you were younger?

_____

_____

Something that I wish everyone knew about me is:

_____

_____

Something about the past that I am glad is over:

_____

_____

Things that I am looking forward to in the future:

_____

_____

_____

write a letter
TO YOUR YOUNGER SELF

Pretend you have a time machine. You travel back into the past and meet your younger self. What do you say? What advice do you give? How do you reassure yourself?

Dear Me,

_____

_____

_____

_____

_____

_____

_____

_____

_____

_____

_____

THE FUTURE IS SO BRIGHT I GOTTA WHERE SHADES DUDE

Future Me

Draw a picture of yourself 10 years from now. What is life like?

JUST FOR LAUGHS

Laughter is good for the soul... Write your favorite jokes here.

_____

_____

_____

_____

_____

_____

_____

_____

_____

_____

_____   _____

_____   _____

_____   _____

_____   _____

The funniest thing that ever happened to me:

_____

_____

_____

_____

_____

_____

_____

The funniest story I ever heard:

_____

_____

_____

_____

_____

_____

_____

small victories

Here is a place to write your accomplishments as you journey to overcome your anxiety. List the little ways you overcame your stresses and worries.

- _____
- _____
- _____
- _____
- _____
- _____
- _____
- _____
- _____
- _____
- _____
- _____
- _____
- _____
- _____
- _____

CELEBRATE YOUR ACCOMPLISHMENTS

What are your three greatest accomplishments?

1. _____
   _____

2. _____
   _____

3. _____
   _____

WHO LOVES ME FOR WHO I AM

_____
_____
_____
_____

HOW I WANT OTHERS TO THINK OF ME

_____
_____
_____
_____
_____
_____
_____

Patience & Perseverance

Have you ever heard the expression, "Good things come to those who wait?" Some things take time, and that's okay. Just because you read a book, gained some knowledge, or tried something new, does not mean your life will instantly change.

Have patience.

Keep a good attitude, while you wait.

Persevere.

Keep trying, even when it's difficult.
If you persevere long enough, you will see results.

SLOW AND STEADY WILL GET YOU THROUGH

And lastly, know that

This too shall pass

That means that you won't always have the problems you are facing now. Life is always changing. Nothing stays the same forever.

The biggest factor in how you feel about your situation is **YOU**.

CHANGE

You are the one thing that can change your situation - even if all you can do is change is the way you *think* about a situation. Changing the way you think about things, can transform your entire life.

Journaling is a good way of expressing yourself, finding solutions, and seeing the progress you have made. The following pages are a place where you can write about your day, track your habits, and more.

- write your affirmation

- color the emoji

- color a sheep for every hour you slept

- color a balloon for an act of kindness you did

- fill in the blanks

- and draw a picture

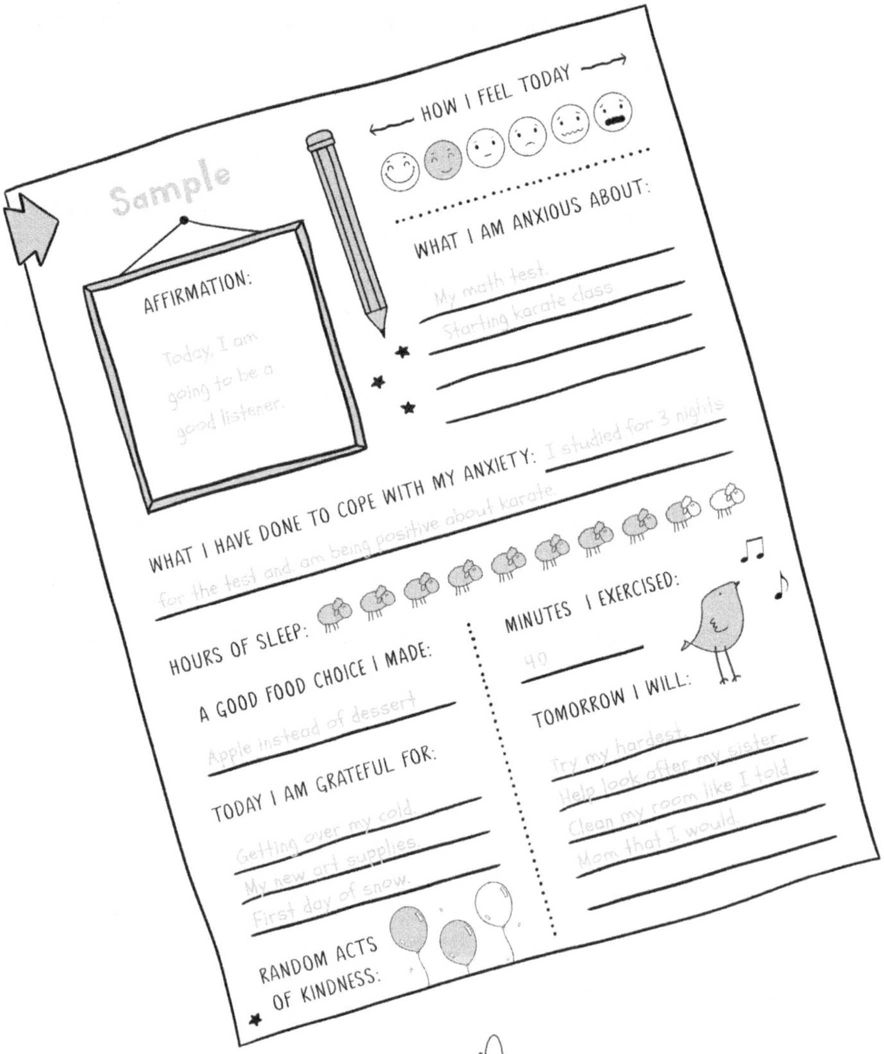

DAILY JOURNAL

Monday

AFFIRMATION:

← HOW I FEEL TODAY →

WHAT I AM ANXIOUS ABOUT:

WHAT I HAVE DONE TO COPE WITH MY ANXIETY:

HOURS OF SLEEP:

A GOOD FOOD CHOICE I MADE:

MINUTES I EXERCISED:

TODAY I AM GRATEFUL FOR:

TOMORROW I WILL:

RANDOM ACTS OF KINDNESS:

JOURNAL ENTRY: _____

TODAY'S DATE:

STUFF TO REMEMBER

Let's get creative! DRAW A PICTURE IN THE BOX.

Tuesday

AFFIRMATION:

← HOW I FEEL TODAY →

WHAT I AM ANXIOUS ABOUT:

WHAT I HAVE DONE TO COPE WITH MY ANXIETY:

HOURS OF SLEEP:

A GOOD FOOD CHOICE I MADE:

MINUTES I EXERCISED:

TODAY I AM GRATEFUL FOR:

TOMORROW I WILL:

RANDOM ACTS OF KINDNESS:

JOURNAL ENTRY: _____

TODAY'S DATE:

STUFF TO REMEMBER

Let's get creative!
DRAW A PICTURE IN THE BOX.

Wednesday

AFFIRMATION:

← HOW I FEEL TODAY →

WHAT I AM ANXIOUS ABOUT:

WHAT I HAVE DONE TO COPE WITH MY ANXIETY:

HOURS OF SLEEP:

A GOOD FOOD CHOICE I MADE:

MINUTES I EXERCISED:

TODAY I AM GRATEFUL FOR:

TOMORROW I WILL:

RANDOM ACTS OF KINDNESS:

JOURNAL ENTRY: _____

TODAY'S DATE:

STUFF TO REMEMBER

Let's get creative! DRAW A PICTURE IN THE BOX.

Thursday

AFFIRMATION:

← HOW I FEEL TODAY →

WHAT I AM ANXIOUS ABOUT:

WHAT I HAVE DONE TO COPE WITH MY ANXIETY:

HOURS OF SLEEP:

A GOOD FOOD CHOICE I MADE:

MINUTES I EXERCISED:

TODAY I AM GRATEFUL FOR:

TOMORROW I WILL:

RANDOM ACTS OF KINDNESS:

JOURNAL ENTRY: _____

_____
_____
_____
_____
_____
_____
_____
_____
_____
_____
_____
_____
_____

TODAY'S DATE:

STUFF TO REMEMBER

_____
_____
_____
_____
_____
_____
_____
_____

Let's get creative! DRAW A PICTURE IN THE BOX.

Friday

AFFIRMATION:

⟵ HOW I FEEL TODAY ⟶

WHAT I AM ANXIOUS ABOUT:

WHAT I HAVE DONE TO COPE WITH MY ANXIETY:

HOURS OF SLEEP:

A GOOD FOOD CHOICE I MADE:

MINUTES I EXERCISED:

TODAY I AM GRATEFUL FOR:

TOMORROW I WILL:

RANDOM ACTS OF KINDNESS:

JOURNAL ENTRY: _____

TODAY'S DATE:

STUFF TO REMEMBER

Let's get creative! DRAW A PICTURE IN THE BOX.

Saturday

AFFIRMATION:

←— HOW I FEEL TODAY —→

WHAT I AM ANXIOUS ABOUT:

WHAT I HAVE DONE TO COPE WITH MY ANXIETY:

HOURS OF SLEEP:

A GOOD FOOD CHOICE I MADE:

MINUTES I EXERCISED:

TODAY I AM GRATEFUL FOR:

TOMORROW I WILL:

RANDOM ACTS OF KINDNESS:

JOURNAL ENTRY: _____

TODAY'S DATE:

STUFF TO REMEMBER

Let's get creative! DRAW A PICTURE IN THE BOX.

Sunday

AFFIRMATION:

← HOW I FEEL TODAY →

WHAT I AM ANXIOUS ABOUT:

WHAT I HAVE DONE TO COPE WITH MY ANXIETY:

HOURS OF SLEEP:

A GOOD FOOD CHOICE I MADE:

MINUTES I EXERCISED:

TODAY I AM GRATEFUL FOR:

TOMORROW I WILL:

RANDOM ACTS OF KINDNESS:

JOURNAL ENTRY: _____

TODAY'S DATE:

STUFF TO REMEMBER

Let's get creative! DRAW A PICTURE IN THE BOX.

Monday

AFFIRMATION:

←— HOW I FEEL TODAY —→

WHAT I AM ANXIOUS ABOUT:

WHAT I HAVE DONE TO COPE WITH MY ANXIETY:

HOURS OF SLEEP:

A GOOD FOOD CHOICE I MADE:

MINUTES I EXERCISED:

TODAY I AM GRATEFUL FOR:

TOMORROW I WILL:

RANDOM ACTS OF KINDNESS:

JOURNAL ENTRY: _____

TODAY'S DATE:

STUFF TO REMEMBER

Let's get creative! DRAW A PICTURE IN THE BOX.

Tuesday

AFFIRMATION:

← HOW I FEEL TODAY →

WHAT I AM ANXIOUS ABOUT:

WHAT I HAVE DONE TO COPE WITH MY ANXIETY:

HOURS OF SLEEP:

A GOOD FOOD CHOICE I MADE:

MINUTES I EXERCISED:

TODAY I AM GRATEFUL FOR:

TOMORROW I WILL:

RANDOM ACTS OF KINDNESS:

JOURNAL ENTRY: _____

TODAY'S DATE:

STUFF TO REMEMBER

Let's get creative! DRAW A PICTURE IN THE BOX.

Wednesday

AFFIRMATION:

← HOW I FEEL TODAY →

WHAT I AM ANXIOUS ABOUT:

WHAT I HAVE DONE TO COPE WITH MY ANXIETY:

HOURS OF SLEEP:

A GOOD FOOD CHOICE I MADE:

MINUTES I EXERCISED:

TODAY I AM GRATEFUL FOR:

TOMORROW I WILL:

RANDOM ACTS OF KINDNESS:

JOURNAL ENTRY: _____

TODAY'S DATE:

STUFF TO REMEMBER

Let's get creative! DRAW A PICTURE IN THE BOX.

Thursday

AFFIRMATION:

← HOW I FEEL TODAY →

WHAT I AM ANXIOUS ABOUT:

WHAT I HAVE DONE TO COPE WITH MY ANXIETY:

HOURS OF SLEEP:

A GOOD FOOD CHOICE I MADE:

MINUTES I EXERCISED:

TODAY I AM GRATEFUL FOR:

TOMORROW I WILL:

RANDOM ACTS OF KINDNESS:

JOURNAL ENTRY: _____

TODAY'S DATE:

STUFF TO REMEMBER

Let's get creative!
DRAW A PICTURE IN THE BOX.

Friday

AFFIRMATION:

← HOW I FEEL TODAY →

WHAT I AM ANXIOUS ABOUT:

WHAT I HAVE DONE TO COPE WITH MY ANXIETY:

HOURS OF SLEEP:

A GOOD FOOD CHOICE I MADE:

MINUTES I EXERCISED:

TODAY I AM GRATEFUL FOR:

TOMORROW I WILL:

RANDOM ACTS OF KINDNESS:

JOURNAL ENTRY: _____

TODAY'S DATE:

STUFF TO REMEMBER

Let's get creative! DRAW A PICTURE IN THE BOX.

Saturday

AFFIRMATION:

← HOW I FEEL TODAY →

WHAT I AM ANXIOUS ABOUT:

WHAT I HAVE DONE TO COPE WITH MY ANXIETY:

HOURS OF SLEEP:

A GOOD FOOD CHOICE I MADE:

MINUTES I EXERCISED:

TODAY I AM GRATEFUL FOR:

TOMORROW I WILL:

RANDOM ACTS OF KINDNESS:

JOURNAL ENTRY: _____

TODAY'S DATE:

STUFF TO REMEMBER

Let's get creative! DRAW A PICTURE IN THE BOX.

Sunday

AFFIRMATION:

← HOW I FEEL TODAY →

WHAT I AM ANXIOUS ABOUT:

WHAT I HAVE DONE TO COPE WITH MY ANXIETY:

HOURS OF SLEEP:

A GOOD FOOD CHOICE I MADE:

MINUTES I EXERCISED:

TODAY I AM GRATEFUL FOR:

TOMORROW I WILL:

RANDOM ACTS OF KINDNESS:

JOURNAL ENTRY: _____

_____
_____
_____
_____
_____
_____
_____
_____
_____
_____
_____
_____
_____

TODAY'S DATE:

STUFF TO REMEMBER

_____
_____
_____
_____
_____
_____
_____

Let's get creative!
DRAW A PICTURE IN THE BOX.

Color Test Page

Test out your markers and pens before you use them. Color in a cloud, then check the back of the page to see if it leaked through.

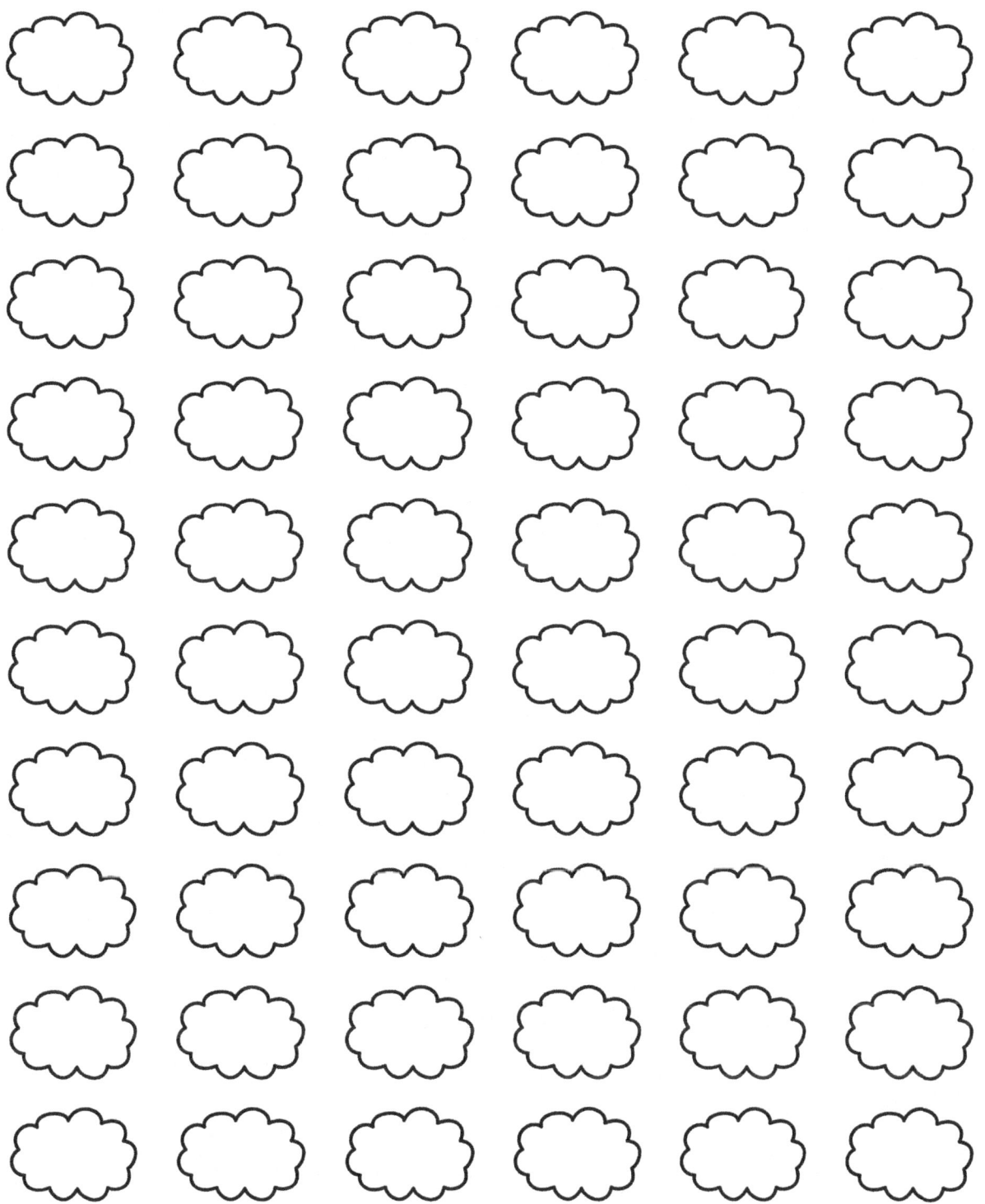

HELP

Never be ashamed or afraid to ask for help.

There are people out there that care about you. If you are in crisis - being abused, or if you have thoughts about hurting yourself there are people here to help.

IN THE U.S.A.
◆ National Alliance on Mental Illness 1-800-950-6264
◆ Teen Line: 1-310-855-HOPE (4673) or 1-800-TLC-TEEN (852-8336)
◆ The Childhelp National Child Abuse Hotline 1-800-422-4453
◆ Girls and Boys Town National Hotline 1-800-448-3000

IN CANADA
◆ Kids Help Phone 1-800-668-6868 or text 686868

If you enjoyed the journal pages at the end of this book and would like more, please have a look at

WORRY FREE ME JOURNAL

Only at Amazon.

©2020 Lina Galanis.

Made in the USA
Monee, IL
18 November 2020